# BOEING 737

## ROBBIE SHAW

# Acknowledgements

I would like to thank the Boeing Airplane Company and my good friend Iain Logan for their assistance with this publication. Unless otherwise credited all photographs were taken by the author using Kodachrome 64 film.

Copyright © Robbie Shaw, 1992
First published in the UK in 1992 by Airlife Publishing Ltd.
ISBN 1 85310 312 8

**British Library Cataloguing in Publication Data available**

A catalogue record for this book is available from the British Library.

Printed in Singapore by Kyodo Printing Co (S'pore) Pte Ltd.

## Airlife Publishing Ltd.

101 Longden Road, Shrewsbury SY3 9EB, England.

# Introduction

Boeing's 727, the first tri-jet in commercial service, became the best selling airliner in the world with a total of 1,832 built, until 19 February 1990 when this title was bestowed on the 'baby' Boeing, as the 1,833rd 737 was rolled out at Boeing's Renton production line. This aircraft, a series -300 was owned by the Australian leasing company Ansett and destined for British Midlands Airways.

The decision to build the 737 short range transport aircraft was announced by Boeing on 19 February 1965, thirty-five years to the day ahead of the record breaking achievement described above. Unlike its twin-engined 'T' tailed competitors, the BAC 1-11 (which had already flown) and the DC-9, Boeing decided on a conventional tail unit with the engines underslung in pods under each wing. The first customer for the 737 was the Federal German carrier Lufthansa, and this was the first occasion that a foreign airline was the launch customer for a US airliner. This variant of the 737 was designated series -100, with a capacity of 100 passengers and powered by two Pratt & Whitney JT8D-1 engines. The prototype took to the air for the first time on 9 April 1967. Deliveries commenced in December of that year. Only thirty series -100s were built, as the series -200 quickly became the standard variant.

Before the prototype had flown Boeing had already announced plans for a larger and more powerful variant, the series -200. The fuselage was lengthened by 1.82 m (six feet) to accommodate up to 130 passengers, whilst improved JT8D engines gave an additional ten per cent thrust. Launch customer for this variant – and the first US airline to order the 737 – was United Airlines who ordered an initial batch of forty aircraft. Indeed the airline's first -200 was received only two days after Lufthansa took delivery of its first series -100 aircraft. Although sales of the 737 were slower than expected, Boeing had faith in their product and announced the -200C/QC, a passenger/cargo variant. The first -200C flew in September 1968 and was delivered to Wien Airlines of Alaska soon afterwards. Over the next two decades the -200 sold in large numbers, particularly when the Advanced -200 was introduced featuring the use of graphite composites to reduce the weight of the airframe, which in turn increased the maximum payload. The last of the 1,114 series -200s was delivered in China in August 1988. Of these nineteen were aircraft destined for the USAF as navigation trainers with the designation T-43A, whilst three special Surveillance variants were acquired by the Indonesian Air Force. These machines are used in both the VIP transport and maritime surveillance roles.

Current 737 production centres on the three 'new generation' variants; the series -300, -400 and -500. The go-ahead for the series -300 was given in March 1981 following orders from US Air and Southwest Airlines for ten aircraft each with options for a further twenty. All 'new generation' 737s are powered by CFM56 engines which are not only more powerful, but considerably quieter than those used on the earlier variants. All three models have a common wing span which is a slight increase on the -200, while the overall height is reduced by six inches. The fuselage of the series -300 has been increased by almost ten feet giving a typical mixed capacity of 128 passengers, with a maximum capacity of 149. These three variants have common two-man cockpits featuring advanced digital avionics and, amazingly, all five versions have identical fuselage width and height. The first series -300 made its maiden flight on 24 February 1984 and soon afterwards Piedmont ordered fifteen of the type. Orders for the -300 were rather sluggish for a couple of years, however, by the end of the decade almost 1,000 aircraft had been ordered. The series -300 is currently the best seller of the three variants available.

The introduction of the series -400 brought an even greater fuselage stretch by a further ten feet to 119 ft 7 in, in a mixed layout this provides seating for 146 passengers, which can be increased to 170 in a charter configuration. The -400 showed the makings of a winner with an initial order for twenty-five aircraft from Piedmont plus the first of many orders from the increasing number of aircraft leasing companies. The 1,000th 'new generation' 737 built was the first -400 for British Airways and was delivered to the airline on 16 October 1991.

In the mid-1980s, although still popular, the series -200 was a twenty-year-old design and, compared with the technology of the -300, becoming outdated. The obvious solution was a variant with the fuselage dimensions of the -200 and the technology of the -300, hence the -500 was born. In May 1987 the type was launched, promising to be twenty-five per cent more fuel efficient than the elderly -200s. The prototype -500 took off from Renton on its maiden flight on 30 June 1989. The first production -500 variant was delivered to Southwest on 28 February the following year, by which time 193 aircraft had been ordered by nineteen airlines.

An important milestone in the career of the Boeing 737 and Lufthansa occurred on 25 February 1991 when the 2,000th 737 built was handed over to the German airline – becoming the 100th 737 Lufthansa had received in twenty-three years. During 1991 Boeing delivered 215 Boeing 737s, setting a record for the most commercial aircraft of a single type to be delivered in a year. At the time of writing, total orders for the 737 family are only a handful short of 3,000, and it is not inconceivable that the figure may eventually reach 4,000. That's not a bad figure for an aircraft of which the manufacturers estimated they would perhaps sell 600!

Robbie Shaw, March 1992.

| TABLE OF COMPARISONS | | |
|---|---|---|
| | -100 | -200 |
| First flight date: | 9 April 1967 | 8 August 1967 |
| Max. accommodation: | 100 | 130 |
| Wing span: | 28.3m (93 ft) | 28.3 m (93 ft) |
| Length: | 28.66 m (94 ft) | 30.53m (100 ft 2 in) |
| Height: | 11.28 m (37 ft) | 11.28 m (37 ft) |
| Max. t/o weight: | 50,350 kg (111,000 lb) | 56,472 kg (124,500 lb) |
| Range with max pax: | 2,945 km (1,830 nm) | 4,179 km (2,255 nm) |
| | -300 | -400 |
| First flight date: | 28 February 1984 | 19 February 1988 |
| Max. accommodation: | 149 | 170 |
| Wing span: | 28.88m (94 ft 9 in) | 28.88 m (94 ft 9 in) |
| Length: | 33.4 m (109 ft 7 in) | 36.4m (119 ft 7 in) |
| Height: | 11.13 m (36 ft 6 in) | 11.13 m (36 ft 6in) |
| Max. t/o weight: | 62,822 kg (138,500 lb) | 68,040 kg (150,000 lb) |
| Range with max pax: | 4,321 km (2,550 nm) | 4,104 km (2,505 nm) |
| | -500 | |
| First flight date: | 30 June 1989 | |
| Max. accommodation: | 132 | |
| Wing span: | 28.88m (94 ft 9 in) | |
| Length: | 31 m (101 ft 9 in) | |
| Height: | 11.13 m (36 ft 6 in) | |
| Max. t/o weight: | 60,550 kg (133,500 lb) | |
| Range with max pax: | 4,683 km (2,805 nm) | |

## AER LINGUS (EI/EIN)

The Irish national carrier is a long established operator of the Boeing 737 and received the first of a batch of eight series -200s in 1969. Over the years the 737 fleet has been steadily expanded, and the airline currently operates over twenty aircraft. Aer Lingus is fairly unique in that it operates the series -200, -300, -400 and -500. Some of the older -200s have been sold while others are used on night freight duties, with the new generation -300 and -400s increasingly been used on high density services to Heathrow, and the -500s to Gatwick. The 737s are also used to serve other European destinations whilst Saab SF340s and Fokker 50s are used on domestic and some UK routes. Three elderly 747s are used on the transatlantic routes whilst two 767s acquired in early 1991 have been leased out. The current livery comprises a dark green window line bordered by a thin bright blue band above, and broad white band below. The belly is grey and the fuselage roof a bright green which encompasses the whole tail, upon which is a large white shamrock. The ICAO callsign is 'SHAMROCK'.

Photographed on approach to runway 27L at Heathrow is B737-300 EI-BUE named 'St Ciara.' (Robbie Shaw)

# AEROMARITIME

French operator Aeromaritime was formed in 1966 to operate charter flights with aircraft leased from UTA. It later became a wholly-owned subsidiary of UTA, and by 1990 was operating a modern fleet of Boeing 737-300s and -400s to European destinations, and 767s for longer range services. During 1991 the airline was, like its parent, taken over by Air France and its aircraft absorbed into that company. Aeromaritime's colour scheme bore a close resemblance to its parent company, with an all white fuselage and, rather unusually, bright green passenger doors. The fin was painted dark blue with a stylised white A' superimposed. Illustrated is Boeing 737-300 F-GFUB. (Author's collection)

## AIR ALGERIE (AH/DAH)

Air Algerie operates a fleet of sixteen 737-200s, the first of which was delivered in 1971 and the last in 1983. These supplement eleven Boeing 727s on routes throughout Europe, whilst Fokker F-27s are used on domestic routes. More recent acquisitions include Airbus A-310s and Boeing 767s which are used to some of the more distant European destinations and on the high density Algiers-Paris/Orly service. Air Algerie's history can be traced to the 1940s when it was known as CGTA, its present title was adopted in 1953 after the take-over of Compagnie Air Transport. Like the state airlines of most ex-French colonies the first jet used by the company was the Sud-

Aviation Caravelle. The present colour scheme was adopted in 1982 and comprises a triple cheatline of two thin red stripes separated by a green one running underneath the window line from nose to tail, gradually thickening as it progresses. The top red line sweeps up to the leading edge of the fin. The fuselage and tail are white with the company logo in red on the fin, and red Air Algerie titling in both English and Arabic on the upper fuselage. The ICAO callsign is 'AIR ALGERIE'.

Boeing 737-200 7T-VEO named 'Titteri' is seen on approach to London's Heathrow airport. (Robbie Shaw)

## AIR ATLANTIS (AIA)

Formed in 1985 as a charter subsidiary of the national carrier TAP-Air Portugal, Air Atlantis initially used 737-200s transferred from that company before eventually acquiring its own. From its main base at Faro the airline operates holiday charters throughout western Europe using three series -200s and four -300s, the first of the latter entering service in 1989 on lease from Bavaria. A further three of the latter variant are on order. The airline's colours are taken from the national flag and feature a thin red and broad green stripe running the length of the fuselage below the window line, with the belly being natural metal. The upper surfaces and tail are white with a red/green stylised 'A' on the fin. The company's ICAO callsign is 'AIR ATLANTIS'.

On short finals to runway 08R at Gatwick is Boeing 737-300 CS-TIH. (Robbie Shaw)

# AIR CALIFORNIA

Air California commenced scheduled services in 1967, concentrating on routes within California, Nevada, Oregon and Washington. In the era of US deregulation the carrier expanded and operated BAe-146s and Boeing 737-200s, later augmented by -300s. The operating name was also shortened to AirCal. In 1987, whilst deliveries of the series -300s were in progress, the airline was taken over by American Airlines who absorbed much of AirCal's fleet onto its own inventory, although a number of 737s were subsequently leased to Braniff. The interesting colour scheme comprised a broad segmented cheatline of mauve, magenta, orange and yellow, which swept up to cover the lower part of the fin, with the remainder of the aircraft painted brilliant white. Photographed at Orange County airport California, is Boeing 737-300 N303AC. (Robbie Shaw)

## AIR EUROPA (UX/AEA)

Air Europa was formed in 1986 to operate inclusive tour charter flights from northern and western Europe to the Spanish resorts on the Balearic and Canary Islands. Long haul flights are also undertaken to North and Central America and the Far East. The airline was closely associated with Air Europe and had an identical livery and fleet, comprising Boeing 737s and 757s. Indeed there was a continual juggling of aircraft between the carriers to meet their respective demands at different times of the year. Despite the demise of Air Europe, the flying operations of Air Europa have not been affected, and the carrier had five 737-300s on strength during 1991. The broad cheatline in varying shades of red and orange runs below the window line and sweeps up the tail, the remainder of the aircraft being white. Air Europa titling in black is featured on the upper fuselage and tail. The airline's ICAO callsign is 'AIR EUROPA'.

Photographed at Geneva is Boeing 737-300 EC-EST. (Robbie Shaw)

## AIR EUROPE

March 1991 was a sad time for British aviation as Air Europe, one of the most promising of the new airlines, ceased operations due to the financial problems of its parent company, the International Leisure Group. The airline started operations from Gatwick in 1979 with charter flights to a number of Europe's favourite holiday destinations, initially using 737-200s. However, an ambitious scheduled network throughout Europe saw the carrier expand and operate a modern fleet of aircraft including 737-200s, -300s and -400s, as well as 757s and Fokker 100s. Even the 747 Jumbo was added to the fleet for transatlantic services, and the airline was one of the first to place orders for MD-11s. A subsidiary, Air Europe Express, used Shorts SD330s and 360s on low density short hop European routes such as Gatwick-Rotterdam, as well as serving the Channel Islands. As mentioned, Air Europe's livery was identical to that of Air Europa. Decelerating after landing at Luton is Boeing 737-300 G-BMTG. (Robbie Shaw)

# AIR FRANCE (AF/AFR)

Air France joined the 737 club in 1982 when the first of an order for twelve series -200s was delivered, these were later joined by a further seven. The airline still operates these aircraft as well as a single -300 leased from Aeromaritime although, since Air France has taken over that company, some of the other -300s have been absorbed into the fleet. During 1991 the first of twelve series -500s were taken on charge. Air France would have liked to take delivery of the 737 much earlier than it did, but there was very strong staff and union opposition to the two-man crew, as previous types operated by the company utilised a flight engineer. With the airline in the process of retiring its Boeing 727s, the 737s support Airbus A-300s, A-310s and A-320s on European services. For long haul routes the airline utilises the Boeing 747, and of course Concorde on the prestigious New York run, whilst a number of A-340s are on order. The current Air France livery was introduced in 1975 and features an all white fuselage with blue titling, whilst the tail is encompassed with blue, white and red tricolour stripes of varying widths. The airline's ICAO callsign is 'AIR FRANCE'.

Taxying for departure at Geneva is Boeing 737-200 F-GFLX. (Robbie Shaw)

## AIR MALTA (KM/AMC)

The Maltese national carrier was formed in 1973 and commenced services with leased Tridents while elderly Boeing 720s were acquired the following year. In 1983 the first Boeing 737-200 was delivered to the airline, which now uses six of these aircraft on both scheduled and charter services to the rest of Europe. Three series -500s are currently on order, with delivery scheduled for 1993, while Airbus A-320s are increasingly used on some routes, including Heathrow. The revised Air Malta livery has a white fuselage with red titling and three thin black stripes on the lower forward fuselage. Most of the fin is red with a white Maltese Cross, and a white lower fin. The ICAO callsign is 'AIR MALTA'.

Photographed on a scheduled service to Heathrow is Boeing 737-200 9H-ABE. (Robbie Shaw)

## AIR NAURU (ON/RON)

The airline of this tiny Pacific island which has a total land area of less than eight square miles was formed in 1970. The first of three 737-200s was delivered in 1975, and services were started to Auckland, Melbourne, Sydney, Taipei and Hong Kong. A fourth machine was added later, but two of these aircraft have since been disposed of, whilst two series -400s are on order and will presumably replace the two aircraft currently in use. The attractive colour scheme has a yellow band along the window line bordered on both sides by dark blue. The upper dark blue band sweeps up to cover the whole of the tail fin where a white twelve pointed star is superimposed, above which is a thin yellow stripe. The remainder of the upper fuselage is white and the lower fuselage grey. The airline's ICAO callsign is 'OSCAR NOVEMBER'.

Photographed lined up for take-off from Hong Kong's Kai Tak airport is Boeing 737-200 C2-RN6. (Robbie Shaw)

## TAP – AIR PORTUGAL (TP/TAP)

Operating under the name Air Portugal, the Portuguese national carrier was until 1979 known as Transportes Aereos Portugueses (TAP). The airline commenced operations from its Lisbon base and now has an extensive route network covering Europe, Africa, North and South America. In the latter continents destinations served include; Boston, Los Angeles, New York, Montreal, Toronto, Caracas, Curacao, Recife, Rio de Janeiro and Sao Paulo, all with Lockheed L-1011 Tristars. The remainder of the network is serviced by Airbus A-310s and Boeing 737s. Of the latter, there are nine series -200 and five -300 aircraft, with a further two -300s on order. The white upper and grey lower fuselage is separated by a thick green and red cheatline which continues halfway up the fin, where the old initials 'TAP' run vertically in red. The 'Air Portugal' titling is in black on the upper fuselage, forward of which is the national flag. The airline's ICAO callsign is 'AIR PORTUGAL'. Photographed taxying to its stand at Frankfurt is Boeing 737-300 CS-TIC 'Algarve'. (Robbie Shaw)

# AIR SINAI (4D/ASD)

A subsidiary of Egyptair, Air Sinai was formed in 1982 to fill the void created when Nefertiti Airlines ceased operations. From its Cairo base the airline uses a couple of Fokker F-27s on some domestic routes, and a Boeing 737-200 leased from Egyptair on the important Cairo-Tel Aviv service. The same aircraft also serves Athens on a daily basis. The colour scheme consists of a gold upper and blue lower cheatline, whilst within a circle on the white fin is an aircraft superimposed over a map containing a gold desert and blue coloured Gulf of Aqaba and Gulf of Suez. The belly is grey and and upper fuselage white, upon which is the airline titling in both English and Arabic. The company ICAO callsign is 'AIR SINAI'.

About to land at Athens is Boeing 737-200 SU-GAN. (Robbie Shaw)

## AIR SUL

Formed as recently as 1989, Air Sul was a Portuguese charter airline based at Lisbon. Operations commenced with a Boeing 737-200 leased from Britannia Airways before it received a pair of its own; former Indian Airlines aircraft leased from Guiness-Peat Leasing. However, in February 1992 after a very short life the airline ceased operations. Air Sul's pleasant colour scheme was based on a natural metal belly and all-white fuselage and tail. Four thin yellow, orange and red stripes run underneath the window line from the nose to the wing, and then broaden and sweep up over the fuselage in the form of a sash. Two yellow and red pendants are located in the centre of the fin with the black figures 'AS'. Air Sul titling, also in black, and the national flag are located on the forward upper fuselage.

Boeing 737-200 CS-TMB named 'Europa' is illustrated at Geneva. (Robbie Shaw)

## ALL NIPPON AIRWAYS (NH/ANA)

Since it was founded in 1952 All Nippon Airways has gradually expanded and is now Japan's largest carrier. The airline was formed under the name Japan Helicopter and Aeroplane Transport Company and, over the next fifteen years, absorbed airlines such as Kyokuto Airlines, Fujita Airlines, Central Japan Airlines and Nagasaki Airways. The company has been known as All Nippon since 1957 and, until 1986, was only permitted to operate domestic services and not to compete with the national carrier Japan Air Lines on international routes. Since that date however the airline has steadily increased its network to include destinations in Asia, Europe and North America. The airline's large fleet consists of YS-11 turboprops, Boeing 737, 747 and 767s, and L-1011 Tristars. When deliveries are completed All Nippon will be the largest operator of the 767, a type which replaced the ageing 727s. The attractive livery has two bands of dark and light blue sweeping diagonally up the fuselage from the nose to encompass the whole fin, all of which, excepting the trailing edge, is dark blue with the letters 'ANA' diagonally in white. The belly is light grey and the remainder of the fuselage white, upon which is the airline titling in Japanese characters only. The ICAO callsign is 'ALL NIPPON'.

The airline currently operates fourteen Boeing 737-200s, including JA8454 seen about to land at Nagoya. (Robbie Shaw)

## ALOHA AIRLINES (AQ/AAH)

Aloha airlines operates an all-Boeing 737 fleet from its base at Honolulu on a network of feeder flights amongst the Hawaiian islands. The airline received its first 737 in the early 1970s and, due to the short flight times between destinations, its aircraft have very high utilisation factors. This became evident on 28 April 1988 when Aloha 737 registration N73711 suffered an amazing in-flight incident when a portion of the fuselage roof and sides peeled back and was torn off. Miraculously the crew managed to land the aircraft safely where amazingly it was found that a stewardess was the only fatality, although not surprisingly a number of passengers were suffering from exposure, shock and injury from flying debris. The cause of this accident was corrosion, and Aloha quickly withdrew from service the three oldest aircraft in its inventory. The airline presently operates thirteen series -200s and two -300s, with a further four of the latter on order. Representing sunshine and sand, Aloha's livery has an orange and yellow cheatline running the length of the fuselage and sweeping up the centre of the fin. The remainder of the fuselage is white with orange titling and the natural metal belly. The ICAO callsign is 'ALOHA'.

On approach to Honolulu is Boeing 737-200 N7376F named 'King Lunaliko'. (Robbie Shaw)

## ASIANA AIRLINES (OZ/AAR)

South Korean carrier Asiana was formed in December 1988 and initially only permitted to operate domestic services. Despite protests from Korean Air this restriction was soon lifted and international routes opened in 1989, initially to Tokyo and Nagoya. Further expansion is planned, to include Europe and North America. The airline acquired ten Boeing 737-400 series aircraft, and has since placed orders for a further thirteen. Two smaller series -500s and two Boeing 767s have also joined the growing fleet.

Asiana has an unusual colour scheme. The lower fuselage and belly is white, the remainder of the aircraft is medium grey. Eight thin lines in red, yellow, blue and white run vertically up the trailing edge of the fin, and the airline titling, in English and Korean characters, is on the upper fuselage. The ICAO callsign is 'ASIANA'.

Taxying at Nagoya for a flight to Seoul is Boeing 737-400 HL 7258. (Robbie Shaw)

# AVIATECA (GU/GUG)

Aviateca – also known as Aerolineas de Guatemala – was formed in 1945 to run domestic air services throughout the country. Since the ageing DC-3s have been disposed of the airline has given up the bulk of these routes. Three Boeing 737-300 and one series -200, all of which are leased, are used to serve Houston, Miami and New Orleans in the USA, and Mexico City. The colour scheme on the 737s comprises a dark blue belly and fin with the remainder of the fuselage painted white. On the fin are five thin horizontal stripes in green, purple, red, orange and yellow. The airline's ICAO callsign is 'AVIATECA'.

Photographed taxying for departure at Miami is Boeing 737-300 N102GU, which is on lease from ILFC. (Robbie Shaw)

## BAHAMASAIR (UP/BHS)

From its Nassau base Bahamasair operates a fleet of Dash-8s and BAe748s on regional services to more than twenty destinations including the Turks and Caicos islands. For destinations further afield, such as Miami and Orlando, three Boeing 737-200s are utilised. The airline's adventurous colour scheme has a yellow cheatline on the lower fuselage to separate the grey belly and white fuselage. The fin is turquoise with a stylised Bahamian flag in yellow and black, whilst yellow bands of varying widths traverse the rear fuselage sash style. The ICAO callsign is 'BAHAMAS'.

Bahamasair run frequent flights to Miami, where Boeing 737-200 C6-BFC was photographed. (Robbie Shaw)

## BALKAN BULGARIAN AIRLINES (LZ/LAZ)

The Bulgarian national carrier was formed with Soviet assistance in 1945 and until 1968 operated as TABSO. The airline has an extensive route network in Europe, and is also well established in Africa and the Middle East. Like the carriers of most Soviet satellite nations the airline operated predominantly Russian-built equipment, however this changed at the end of 1990 when two Boeing 737-500s were acquired on lease, and a year later the first of four Airbus A-320s. The airline's current livery which was adopted in 1985 has an all-white fuselage with red and green stripes running three-quarters of the length of the fuselage from the nose. The same stripes run vertically up the fin with the red Balkan titling on the fuselage in English on the starboard side and Slavic on the port. Balkan's ICAO callsign is 'BALKAN'.

Photographed at (East) Berlin's Schonefeld airport soon after entering service is Boeing 737-500 LZ-BOB 'City of Plovdiv'. (Robbie Shaw)

## BRAATHENS SAFE AIR TRANSPORT (BU/BRA)

This independent Norwegian carrier was formed in 1946 to operate long haul charter flights, though a scheduled service was opened to Hong Kong in 1949 which was taken over by SAS in 1954. The initials SAFE stand for South American and Far East, but these days the airline's scheduled network is restricted to Northern Europe. In addition to inclusive charters Braathens operates a number of domestic routes and a few scheduled services including a new Oslo-London/Gatwick service. The airline is a long established 737 operator having operated the type since 1971. The large fleet of series -200 aircraft is slowly being disposed of as the series -500s, twenty-five of which are on order, are delivered. There are also four larger -400 series aircraft on strength with two more on order. The Braathens livery has remained unchanged for many years and consists of a natural metal belly and white fuselage separated by a red and black stripe below the window line. The white fin contains the Norwegian flag. The ICAO callsign is 'BRAATHENS'.

Boeing 737-200 LN-SUA named 'Harald Svarte' rotates from the runway at Geneva. (Robbie Shaw)

## BRITANNIA AIRWAYS (BY/BAL)

Britannia Airways was the first European airline to operate the Boeing 737 when it put the type into service in 1968, and at one time the airline had over thirty series -200s in use. In 1992 this number has been reduced to twenty and will be reduced further as deliveries of the Boeing 757s and 767s on order are completed. Britannia also had six 737-300s which it acquired when it took over Orion Airways, although ideally it would like to dispose of these aircraft, and one has recently gone to Dan Air. Britannia's charter network spreads all over the globe and is one of which any large airline would be proud. There is hardly a country in Europe in which Britannia aircraft are not a common sight, whilst the airline operates more flights to Orlando Florida than any non-US airline. The Caribbean, Africa, Australia and New Zealand are all served frequently by the airline's fleet of 767s, whilst a daily scheduled service with high load factors is operated from its Luton base to Belfast. The current Britannia colour scheme was adopted in 1983 and comprises a dark blue belly with five white pinstripes running the length of the fuselage and gradually widening as they proceed upwards, stopping below the window line. The remainder of the fuselage is white with dark blue Britannia titling, forward of which is the silhouette of the head of Queen Boadicea. The fin is dark blue with the white pinstripes at the base, this time widening as they proceed downwards. Superimposed on the dark blue fin is the figure of Queen Boadicea in white holding a Union flag shield. The airline's ICAO callsign is 'BRITANNIA'.

Photographed a split second from touchdown at Luton is Boeing 727-200 G-BAZG named 'Florence Nightingale'. (Robbie Shaw)

## BRITISH AIRWAYS (BA/BAW)

A strong supporter of Boeing products, British Airways has operated the 737 since 1980. An initial batch of nineteen was received, which was increased to the present total of over forty series -200s. These were later joined by four -300s on lease from the Danish airline Maersk. To replace its fleet of BAC 1-11s and some of the series -200s British Airways selected the 737-400, and the first of twenty-four on order was delivered on 16 October 1991. This particular aircraft was the 1,000th 'new generation' 737 built by Boeing. The 737 has been used by the airline almost exclusively on its European network, as well as a few domestic routes such as Jersey. When the BAC-111s have been sold, of the airline's inventory of over 200 aircraft, only the small number of ATPs, BAe748s, DC-10s, A-320s and Concorde in use will not be Boeing products. The airline's colour scheme consists of a midnight blue lower fuselage and belly with a red 'speedwing' running almost the entire length of the plane. The upper fuselage is pearl grey with midnight blue titling. The top half of the fin is midnight blue, within which is the airline's coat of arms in pearl grey. The lower half of the fin is also pearl grey with a quartered Union flag. The ICAO callsign is 'SPEEDBIRD'.

Brand new Boeing 737-400 G-DOCD 'River Aire' is seen about to land at Heathrow on Christmas Eve 1991. (Robbie Shaw)

## BRITISH MIDLAND AIRWAYS (BD/BMA)

British Midland is a strong independent carrier with an expanding network of scheduled services throughout Europe and a deserved reputation for its 'Diamond Class' service. Based at East Midlands airport, the airline operates ATPs and Dash-7s on short range domestic sectors, while a larger number of DC-9s and Boeing 737s are used on European and longer range domestic routes. The airline provides strong competition to British Airways on the high density Heathrow to Glasgow, Edinburgh and Belfast routes using 737s. British Midland received its first series -300 in 1987 and currently operates seven of this variant and three larger -400s. At weekends during the summer DC-9s are often used on the

Heathrow routes mentioned earlier, thereby releasing the greater capacity 737s for IT charter work. The airline livery has a thin white cheatline separating the lower fuselage and belly, which are light grey, from the rest of the aircraft which is royal blue. The company logo consisting of a red 'BM' with a grey diamond is located on the fin and repeated slightly smaller on the forward fuselage ahead of the white titling. The ICAO radio callsign is 'MIDLAND'.

Boeing 737-300 G-OBMJ is almost shrouded in spray as it decelerates after landing on a rain soaked Jersey runway. (Robbie Shaw)

## CANADIAN AIRLINES INTERNATIONAL (CP/CDN)

Canadian Airlines International was the result of a merger between Canadian Pacific and Pacific Western, two of Canada's largest independent carriers. Since that merger the airline has also taken over Wardair and that company's Airbus A-310s and international routes, including a successful London/Gatwick service. Canadian now provides serious competition to Air Canada on both the domestic and international fronts. Canadian's extensive international network includes Buenos Aires, Lima, Mexico City, Rio de Janeiro, Santiago and Sao Paula in South America, with Bangkok, Beijing, Hong Kong, Shanghai, Taipei and Tokyo in the Far East. Steady expansion in Europe continues, including Amsterdam, Frankfurt, Milan and Paris, with Auckland and Sydney in Australasia. Within Canada a small number of feeder airlines operate under the 'Canadian Partner' system in full Canadian livery. As a result of the merger Canadian had at one time more than seventy Boeing 737-200s on its inventory, though with deliveries of the substantial number of A-320s on order this has been reduced to just over fifty. The attractive airline livery has the aircraft belly and engines in deep blue, with a thin red and grey cheatline below the window line leading to the off-white fuselage. The airline's logo of a large red arrowhead and four deep blue pinstripes on a grey background occupies the centre of the fin, the remainder of which is deep blue. The logo in reduced size is rather cleverly included in the titling on the upper fuselage thus, 'CANADI>N', thereby avoiding the issue of whether to use the English or French spelling. The ICAO callsign is 'CANADIAN'.

Photographed on departure from Toronto is Boeing 737-200 C-GRCP. (Robbie Shaw)

## CAYMAN AIRWAYS (KX/CAY)

Cayman Airways was formed in 1968 as a subsidiary of the Costa Rican carrier LACSA, but in 1977 became wholly government-owned. From its base at George Town, Grand Cayman, inter-island services are undertaken using a Shorts SD330 whilst Boeing 737s are used on the increasing number of scheduled services, particularly to the USA. In Florida, Miami and Tampa are served by frequent services, whilst Houston and New York have recently been added to the network which also includes Kingston, Jamaica. In 1992 the airline has four 737s; two -400s with one more on order and one -200,

all of which are leased. The bellies of the aircraft are painted deep blue, with white, red and green pinstripes running the length of the fuselage below the window line, the remainder of the fuselage is white. Rather unusually the same scheme is repeated on the engines of the 737s. On the white fin is a caricature of a 'pirate' turtle complete with hat, cutlass and peg-leg. The airline's ICAO callsign is 'CAYMAN'.

Taxying onto the runway at Miami is Boeing 737-400 VR-CAB. (Robbie Shaw)

## CHINA AIRLINES (CI/CAL)

A strong supportter of Boeing products is Taiwan's China Airlines. The carrier commenced operations in 1962 with piston engined DC-3s, DC-4s and C-46s. The first jets were introduced in 1967 with the acquisition of Boeing 727s, quickly followed by 707s. All these aircraft have since been disposed of, the 727s to the air force and the 707s sold. The airline has a strong regional network for which the popular Airbus A-300s are used. Two Boeing 767s were also used on these routes, but have since been disposed of in favour of more A-300s. For long range services to Europe and the USA

Boeing 747s are used, including the SP variant. Only a few domestic routes are undertaken, using three Boeing 737-200s which were acquired from 1986. China Airlines' colour scheme consists of a red, white and blue cheatline, with the same colours running vertically up the centre of the fin. Lower surfaces are grey, and on the white upper surfaces is blue titling in both English and Chinese. The ICAO callsign is 'DYNASTY'.

Taxying to a stop at its stand at Taipei's Chiang Kai Shek international airport is Boeing 737-200 B-182. (Robbie Shaw)

# CIVIL AVIATION ADMINISTRATION of CHINA (CAAC)/CHINA SOUTHERN (CA/CSN)/ CHINA EASTERN (CA/CES)

Another strong supporter of Boeing products is the national airline of the 'other' China, the People's Republic. Until recently the airline was known as CAAC – Civil Aviation Administration of China. However, liberalisation has meant a move to regional airlines, and CAAC has been split up. Airlines with 'inspiring' names such as China Eastern, China Southern, China Southwest, China Northwest and Air China now operate throughout the country, although it will be some time before all former CAAC aircraft are painted in their new liveries. Soviet-built aircraft such as the An-24, Il-18 and Tu-154s are still used on domestic routes alongside the locally built YUN-7 – a licence built An-24. An increasing number of western-built airlines are now in use, including British-built SD330s, BAe-146s and Tridents, whilst US types are the Boeing 707, 737, 747, 757 and 767. The Airbus A-300s and A-310s remain in use, whilst McDonnell-Douglas MD-80s are built under licence in China. As mentioned, most aircraft still wear the CAAC livery which has a blue cheatline separating the white upper and grey lower fuselage. The white fin contains a large Chinese flag, and the airline titling – in Chinese characters only – is in black on the upper fuselage. The CAAC callsign was 'CHINA', and the new companies are 'CHINA SOUTHERN' etc.

A total of sixteen Boeing 737-200s were acquired by CAAC. The last of these, B-2516, is illustrated landing at Shanghai's Hongqiao airport in 1987, and has since been transferred to China Southern airlines based at Guanghzou (Canton). (Robbie Shaw)

In addition to the series -200s, CAAC also acquired eight -300s, with a larger batch in the process of being delivered, while fifteen series -500s are being produced for China Southern. Photographed about to land at Hong Kong's Kai Tak airport is Boeing 737-300 B-2532. This aircraft now operates with Air China, the carrier which undertakes international flights. (Robbie Shaw)

## CONTINENTAL AIRLINES (CO/COA)

As the saying goes, everything in Texas is big, and Houston based Continental Airlines is no exception, being the fourth largest US carrier. Since it formed in 1937 the airline has continued to expand and in the past decade has taken over Texas International Airlines, Frontier Airlines, New York Air and People Express. An extensive domestic network now comprises over seventy destinations, whilst international routes include Australia, New Zealand, Mexico, Canada, Japan, Micronesia and Tahiti, with London and Paris being the only European destinations. An extensive feeder service is operated under the Continental Express banner, and these are provided by: Britt Airways, Bar Harbour and Rocky Mountain Airways. The airline's fleet comprises nearly 100 examples each of the Boeing 727, 737 and DC-9/MD80, along with smaller number of the A-300, Boeing 747 and DC-10. The 737 inventory includes a small number of elderly former People's Express series -100 aircraft, thirty -200s and sixty-two -300s, with a further fifty of the latter on order. Continental's colourful livery comprises a white fuselage bisected by an orange, red and gold cheatline, with the gold continuing up to encompass the fin. The airline circle motif on the fin is in red with the fuselage titling in red. The airline's ICAO callsign is 'CONTINENTAL'.

Photographed at Buffalo, New York is Boeing 737-100 N77215. This aircraft is a former Lufthansa and People's Express machine. (Robbie Shaw)

## COPA PANAMA (CM/CMP)

Compania Panamena de Aviacon (COPA) is the Panamanian national airline which was formed in 1944 by Pan-America but is now Panamanian owned. Regional services are undertaken within the Central American basin, and to Kingston, Jamaica and Miami, Florida. The airline has a small fleet of two Boeing 737s, one a series -100 and the other a -200, a Boeing 727 operated previously has been returned to the lessor. The colour scheme has a twin cheatline of red and orange which then runs vertically up the centre of the fin, where it is interrupted by the red COPA logo. The remainder of the aircraft is white with a natural metal belly. The COPA Panama titling on the upper fuselage is in red and blue alongside the national flag. The ICAO callsign is 'COPA'.

Entering the runway at Miami is Boeing 737-100 HP-873-CMP, an aircraft which once belonged to Air Florida. (Robbie Shaw)

## DAN-AIR SERVICES (DA/DAN)

Dan-Air is a long established independent scheduled and charter carrier which was formed in 1953. When operations were first started the company had a diverse collection of aircraft, including an Avro York and Airspeed Ambassadors, and in later years was one of the final operators of the Comet 4. During 1991 a rationalisation programme was begun, with the airline planning a steady expansion of scheduled services within Europe and less dependence upon holiday charters. Similarly a steady fleet modernisation programme was started, with some Boeing 727s and BAC 1-11s available for sale, to be replaced by new generation Boeing 737s. Dan-Air's fleet currently stands at some fifty aircraft, including BAe-748s, BAe-146s, BAe-111s, and Boeing 727s and 737s. During

the first quarter of 1992 a number of new generation 737s were acquired, and the 737 fleet currently comprises; four -200s, three -300s and eight -400s. During 1992 scheduled services are planned to link Gatwick with Athens, Istanbul, Rome and Stockholm, all of which will feature the airline's quality 'Class Elite' service to business travellers. The company livery has thin red and blue cheatlines running from the nose, gradually broadening and sweeping up to encompass the tail. Also on the tail is a large white disc containing the company logo of a compass and pennant. The Dan-Air London titling is in blue on a white upper fuselage. The company's ICAO callsign is 'DAN-AIR'. Climbing out of Gatwick is Boeing 737-400 G-BNNL. (Robbie Shaw)

## DELTA AIRLINES (DL/DAL)

Atlanta-based Delta Airlines is one of America's megacarriers with a fleet of almost 400 aircraft, 129 of which are Boeing 727s. The airline has a large domestic network serving no less than 240 US destinations, and has recently expanded European services. At the time of writing Delta can boast over 4,800 flights a day to 300 destinations in thirty-three countries – quite an achievement. Most international routes are operated by Lockheed L-1011 Tristars supported by Boeing 767-300ERs, but no doubt the thirteen MD-11s being delivered will be employed on such routes. Domestic services are catered for by the large 727 fleet and MD-88s, as well as eighty-four Boeing 757s, making Delta the second largest operator of the 757. These are supported by a sizeable fleet of Boeing 737s, fifty-nine of which are series -200s with a total of seventy -300s in service and on order. Delta's colour scheme has a dark blue cheatline which extends to wrap around the nose, and has upper trimming in the form of a red pinstripe. Almost all of the fin is taken up by the large dark blue and red delta shapes which form the company logo, and are repeated in smaller size just behind the cockpit. The remainder of the aircraft is white apart from highly polished natural metal undersurfaces. The ICAO callsign is 'DELTA'. About to land at Detroit Metropolitan airport is Boeing 737-200 N378DL. (Robbie Shaw)

# DRAGONAIR (HONG KONG DRAGON AIRLINES) (KA/HDA)

Dragonair was formed in late 1985 with the plan to start services from Hong Kong to a number of regional destinations within the People's Republic of China. Two Boeing 737-200s were acquired, however, during the first year of operation much of their time was spent on the ground due to strong opposition from Cathay Pacific, and only occasional charter flights were undertaken. Over the next few years a few scheduled routes were awarded to the airline and a third aircraft purchased. Eventually in 1990 an agreement was reached with Cathay and its parent company Swire Pacific, who took a thirty per cent holding in the fledgling airline. Dragonair currently operates five 737-200s and an L-1011 Tristar leased from Cathay Pacific. The Dragonair colour scheme has a bright orange cheatline, within which is a white pinstripe running the length of the aircraft from the tip of the nose. The orange stripe sweeps up as it progresses towards the rear fuselage and encompasses the whole fin, upon which is a golden dragon. The remainder of the aircraft is white, with small gold titling on the forward fuselage in both English and Chinese characters. The ICAO callsign is 'LOONGAIR'.

On short finals to Kai Tak airport is Boeing 737-200 VR-HYK. The aircraft's registration is in recognition of the now deceased Sir Y.K. Pao, who was a major shareholder. (Robbie Shaw)

## EGYPTAIR (MS/MSR)

One of the oldest airlines in the Middle East is Egyptair, though it has only been known by its present title since 1971. When formed in Cairo in 1932 it operated under the title Misrair Airwork, then becoming just Misrair then United Arab Airlines. When services to Europe commenced British aircraft in the shape of Viscounts and Comet 4Cs were used, however during the honeymoon period with the USSR a number of Soviet types were acquired. These include An-24s, Il-18s and Il-62s, and Tu-154s, though a number of 707s and 737s were purchased from Boeing. The Soviet equipment – which was never popular – has since been disposed of in favour of an all-western fleet. Fokker F-27s and Boeing 737s predominate on domestic and some regional routes, with Airbus A-300s and Boeing 767s used on most international services, supported by two Boeing 747s on long haul routes. Egyptair currently has six 737-200s with five -500s being delivered. The colour scheme has a white fuselage with a broad red cheatline running along the window-line and a thinner gold line underneath. Within a gold disc on the white fin is the company logo – the head of Horus, a falcon-headed god of ancient Egypt, in a vivid red and black. The black titling is in both English and Arabic letters. The ICAO callsign is 'EGYPTAIR'.

As dusk approaches Boeing 737-200 SU-AYI approaches Athens. (Robbie Shaw)

## EUROBERLIN FRANCE (EE/EEB)

EuroBerlin France was formed in late 1988 to operate services from Berlin/Tegel airport. The airline is jointly owned by Air France and Lufthansa, with Luton-based Monarch Airlines contracted to supply its fleet of Boeing 737-300s, four of which were supplied initially. This number has since been increased to eight, and destinations served include Cologne/Bonn, Dusseldorf, Frankfurt, Hamburg, Munich, Nuremburg and Stuttgart. The simple colour scheme features an all-white aircraft except for a disc on the fin, the upper half of which is blue, the lower half red. Blue and red titling is on the upper fuselage. The ICAO callsign is 'EUROBER'.

Photographed taxying to its stand at Frankfurt is Boeing 737-300 G-MONH. (Robbie Shaw)

# FAR EASTERN AIR TRANSPORT (EF/FEA)

Far Eastern Air Transport (FAT) was formed in 1957 and, until 1965, was engaged solely in charter operations. From that year scheduled domestic and international services were operated, however nowadays only the former feature on the airline's network. From its base at Taipei's Sungshan airport FAT serves Hualien, Kaohsiung, Makung, Tainan and Taitung using a fleet of six Boeing 737-200s and two series -100s. Two ATR-72s are on order for imminent delivery. The airline's livery has a red cheatline separating the white upper

fuselage from the natural metal lower fuselage and belly. The red and black titling in English and Chinese characters runs the length of the upper fuselage, whilst the white fin has a red leading-edge chevron and small Taiwanese flag.

About to land at Taipei/Sungshan airport in the suburbs of the capital is Boeing 737-100 B-2621, a former Lufthansa veteran. (Robbie Shaw)

## FUTURA (FH/FUA)

Futura is a Spanish charter operator set up by Aer Lingus with Spanish financial backing and commenced operations in February 1990. From its base at Palma the airline utilises four Boeing 737-400s leased from Guiness-Peat, and IT charters are undertaken to Eire and other European countries. The pleasant colour scheme is based on a white fuselage with red and yellow bands sweeping upwards from the forward belly and running underneath the window-line to the tail. The yellow band expands and sweeps upwards to encompass the tail, upon which is the logo of the blue and red planets orbiting. The red Futura titling is on the forward fuselage with a reduced sized logo. The ICAO callsign is 'FUTURA'.

Entering the apron at Zurich's Kloten airport is Boeing 737-400 EC-EVE. (Robbie Shaw)

## GB AIRWAYS (GT/GBL)

GB Airways, formerly known as Gibraltar Airways and Gibair has joint bases at Gibraltar and Gatwick, from where five Boeing 737-200s are operated to a number of destinations in southern Spain and North Africa. Two of these aircraft have recently been acquired from British Airways to cope with the expanding route network. The airline also operates the shortest intercontinental route in the world, from Gibraltar to Tangier, linking Europe with Africa in less than fifteen minutes. At weekends the fleet of aircraft are kept busy on holiday charter flights; skiing in Switzerland in winter and Spanish beaches in the summer. The stylish colour scheme features an all-white aircraft with a mid-blue and orange cheatline commencing just below the nose, these colours are separated by a thin white stripe. The colours are repeated horizontally across the middle of the fin with the company logo superimposed. The logo comprises a red diamond, the left half of which has five white horizontal lines. The logo is also featured on the cheatline immediately aft of the cockpit, with the red and orange titling on the forward fuselage. The ICAO callsign is 'GIBAIR.'

Looking immaculate, the appropriately registered Boeing 737-200 G-IBTY awaits its passengers at Geneva during the ski holiday season. (Robbie Shaw)

# GULF AIR (GF/GFA)

Gulf Air was set up as the national carrier for the Arabian (Persian) Gulf States of Bahrain, Oman, Qatar and the United Arab Emirates, however in 1985 the latter country set up its own carrier, Emirates Airlines. The airline was first formed in Bahrain in 1950 as Gulf Aviation and commenced regional services with an Avro Anson, before taking delivery of a Dove and Herons. These were later followed by DC-3s and Fokker F-27s. The first jet selected was the BAC-111, followed by VC-10s leased from the then BOAC. Currently, Gulf Air uses ten Boeing 737-200s on regional routes with

Lockheed L-1011 Tristars and Boeing 767s on international services to Europe and the Far East. The colour scheme comprises a white fuselage with three bands in purple, green and red from the nose to the wing root, gradually thinning as they proceed aft. The same colours cover the top half of the fin, this time in vertical format. The lower fin is white with a golden falcon superimposed, whilst gold titling in English and Arabic is on the upper fuselage. The ICAO callsign is 'GULF AIR'.

About to land at Athens is Boeing 737-200 A40-BE. (Robbie Shaw)

## ICELANDAIR (FI/ICE)

Icelandair, the Icelandic national carrier was formed in 1973 through a merger of Icelandair (Flugfelag Islands) and Loftleidir, and operates both international and domestic services. The latter are operated under the title Flugleidir from Reykjavik airport using Fokker F-27s, though Fokker 50s are on order as replacements. International services cannot be operated from Reykjavik airport due to its close proximity to the city centre and inadequate runway length, and instead use the NATO base at Keflavik fifty kilometres away, where a new terminal building has been built. European routes are served by four Boeing 737-400s whilst two Boeing 757s fly

to Baltimore, New York and Orlando, as well as supplementing the 737s on European routes. The simple colour scheme has an all-white fuselage with a mid-blue cheatline and black titling, with the same blue covering the lower part of the engines. The airline's stylised blue 'F' is located midway up the white fin. The ICAO callsign is 'ICEAIR'.

Taxying for departure at Glasgow/Abbotsinch airport for a scheduled flight to Keflavik is Boeing 737-400 TF-FIB 'Eydis'. (Robbie Shaw)

## INTER EUROPEAN AIRWAYS (IP/IEA)

This Cardiff-based charter operator was formed in 1986 as a subsidiary of Aspro holidays and commenced operations in 1987 with leased Boeing 737-200s. These were replaced the following year by series -300 aircraft on long term lease from Guiness-Peat, and the airline now has four such aircraft and a single 757. The bulk of the airline's operations are from Bristol and Cardiff to a variety of holiday destinations around Europe. The two pairs of cheatlines along the lower fuselage in red, yellow and white give the aircraft a 'candy' striped appearance. The cheatlines sweep up the trailing edge of the white fin which contains the stylised initials IEA. The upper fuselage is white with black titling and the belly of the aircraft brown. The fuselage colour scheme is repeated on the engine cowlings. The airline's ICAO callsign is 'ASPRO', in deference to its parent company.

Taxying for departure at Geneva's Cointrin airport during the ski holiday season is Boeing 737-300 G-IEAA. (Robbie Shaw)

## ISTANBUL AIRLINES (IL/IST)

Due to the expansion of tourism in Turkey, Istanbul Airlines was formed in 1986 to operate charter flights, principally from Germany but also from other European countries. Initial equipment comprised a few ageing noisy Sud-Aviation Caravelles, and these aircraft were still in use during 1991. More modern equipment in the shape of three Boeing 737-400s has now been acquired with two -300s also on order. With the introduction of the 737s scheduled services are now undertaken to Amsterdam, Cologne, Hamburg and Munich. The colour scheme is based on a white fuselage and a deep-blue belly,

with blue and red pinstripes separating the two. Red titling is on the forward fuselage whilst the company's red tulip style motif is on the white fin. At the time of writing however, it appears that a slight change is underway, as at least one aircraft now sports a dark blue fin with the company motif within a white circle. The ICAO callsign is 'ISTANBUL'.

About to land at Gatwick is Boeing 737-400 TC-ADA named 'Lale'. (Robbie Shaw)

# J.A.T. – JUGOSLOVENSKI AEROTRANSPORT (JU/JAT)

The Yugoslav national carrier commenced operations in 1947 using ex-wartime Junkers Ju-52s, although over the next decade aircraft such as the DC-3, Convair 340 and 440, Ilyushin Il-14 and Douglas DC-6 were acquired and routes opened to western Europe. The first jet equipment, in the shape of the Caravelle, arrived in the late 1960s, followed by DC-9s and Boeing 727s. The latter two types are still in use on the European network alongside nine Boeing 737-300s which were delivered from 1985 onwards. Four DC-10s are used on intercontinental routes whilst MD-11s are on order as replacements.

The livery on the 737s, rather unusually, has a natural metal fuselage with a red/white/blue cheatline below the window line. The blue fin contains a red circle outlined in white within which are the white letters JAT. The airline titling in red on the upper fuselage has 'Yugoslav Airlines' on the starboard and 'Jugoslovenski Aerotransport' on the port side. The ICAO callsign is 'YUGOSLAV'.

On final approach to runway 23 at Glasgow's Abbotsinch airport on a scheduled flight from Ljubljana is Boeing 737-300 YU-ANK. (Robbie Shaw)

## K.L.M. – ROYAL DUTCH AIRLINES (KL/KLM)

At the time of writing negotiations had just broken down between KLM and British Airways about a merger which, had it gone ahead, would have made the joint carrier the strongest and largest airline in Europe. The initials KLM stand for Koninklijke Luchtvaart Maatschappij (Royal Dutch Airlines) and it is the oldest airline in the world still operating under its original name. Since being formed in 1919 the airline has steadily expanded with a very extensive route network. It was the first airline in Europe to operate the DC-3, and has since been a strong supporter of Douglas products using DC-6, DC-7, DC-8, DC-9 and DC-10 aircraft, and with MD-11s on order. Presently Boeing 737s and A-310s are used on the European network with DC-10s and Boeing 747s on the intercontinental routes.

Boeing 737 deliveries commenced in 1986 to replace the DC-9s, and the current fleet consists of thirteen series -300s with a further three on order, and six -400s with four more on order. In addition a few -200s have occasionally been leased from Transavia. The modern colour scheme has a deep blue cheatline along the windows separated from the grey lower fuselage by a white stripe. The upper fuselage is a pleasant light blue with white KLM titling and crown logo near the forward door. The white tail has the same titling and logo, in dark and light blue respectively. The ICAO callsign is 'KLM'. PH-BDS named 'Joris van Spilbergen' is a Boeing 737-400, and was photographed about to land at Heathrow. (Robbie Shaw)

## LAUDA AIR (NG/LDA)

Named after the famous grand prix racing driver who formed the airline and is still a major shareholder, Lauda Air commenced charter operations in 1979 using two F-27s. Jet equipment arrived at the end of 1985 in the shape of a Boeing 737-200 leased from Transavia, with the airline's first series -300 arriving the following year. Scheduled services commenced in 1988, and Lauda now has a daily Vienna-Gatwick service in conjunction with Dan-Air, whilst Boeing 767s frequent routes to the Far East. One of the 767s was lost in tragic circumstances in May 1991 soon after take-off from Bangkok but is to be replaced, and the ambitious airline has already ordered four Boeing 777s. In addition to the series -300 aircraft

Lauda has one -400, with a further two on order. The colour scheme comprises a double red pinstripe below the window-line separating the cabin, which is white, from the dark grey lower fuselage and belly. The dark grey stops just in front of the rear door leaving the rear fuselage all white, whilst a single red pinstripe runs along the grey at wing root level. The white tail is almost completely taken up by a large red reversed 'L' logo. Red Lauda titling is on the forward upper fuselage and the engine cowlings are white. The airline's ICAO callsign is 'LAUDA AIR'.

On final approach to Gatwick is Boeing 737-300 OE-ILG. (Robbie Shaw)

# LUFTHANSA (LH/DLH)

The airline which started the 737 story back in 1965 still operates a large fleet of this successful twin-jet, and will soon be able to claim that it has operated every variant of the type. The elderly series -100s have long been disposed of and the -200s are in the process of being replaced by the -500, forty-two of which will soon be on strength. Twenty-eight -300 series are in use, the first of these was delivered in 1986 and, although no -400s are yet in use, seven are on order. The remainder of the Lufthansa fleet consists of A-300s, A-310s, A-320s, DC-10s and Boeing 747s, whilst nine A-330s and fifteen A-340s are on order. A small number of 727s remain but are rapidly being replaced by the A-320. The present colour scheme features an all-white fuselage, except for the belly from the wing root downwards, which is grey. The dark blue tail has a yellow circle within which is the company stylised flying crane motif. Dark blue Lufthansa titling is on the forward fuselage. The airline's ICAO callsign is 'LUFTHANSA'.

With the influx of series -500s they are becoming a common sight at European airports, including Heathrow, where D-ABIW was seen. (Robbie Shaw)

## LUXAIR (LG/LGL)

The national carrier of the tiny Grand Duchy of Luxembourg was formed in 1962 and, using a leased Fokker F-27, services were started to Amsterdam, Frankfurt and Paris. Since then the network has expanded somewhat, although the only points served outside Europe are Johannesburg and Nairobi. Fokker F-27s are still used for short range routes supported by Fokker 50s, whilst Boeing 737s are used to other European destinations, and a Boeing 747SP leased from South African Airways used to that continent. Two Boeing 737-

200s were acquired from 1977-8 and a third on lease from Sabena in 1988. Two each of the series -400 and -500 are on order. The livery has a white upper and grey lower fuselage separated by a light blue cheatline. The tail is light blue with a white stylised 'L' logo. Black titling and national flag appear on the upper fuselage. The ICAO callsign is 'LUXAIR'.

Featured against a menacing sky is Boeing 737-200 LX-LGN, formerly OO-SDA and leased from Sabena. (Robbie Shaw)

## MAERSK AIR (DM/DMA)

Formed in 1969, Maersk Air is a subsidiary of the A. P. Moller (Maersk Line) Group well known in shipping circles. The airline was set up to undertake inclusive tour charters, principally to Europe's main sunshine holiday areas, and initially used Boeing 720s. The airline now operates domestic services within Denmark, and has recently expanded to international scheduled flights. These include flights to Gatwick from Billund and Copenhagen. The former are mostly undertaken with Fokker 50s and the latter with Boeing 737s, the latter are also utilised for charter work. The first series -200 737s were acquired in 1976, but have since been disposed of in favour of ten -300s and five -500s, with one more -300

on order. The 737s are also frequently leased to other carriers, including four -300s leased to British Airways until that carrier received its -400s. Maersk's attractive colour scheme is based on overall light blue with twin medium and dark blue cheatline trimmed in white below the window line. The white seven pointed star motif is featured on the fin outlined by a white square. The white titling and smaller motif are on the forward upper cabin. The airline's ICAO callsign is 'MAERSKAIR'.

Illustrated is Boeing 737-500 OY-MAD. (Robbie Shaw)
(Robbie Shaw)

## MALAYSIA AIRLINES (MH/MAS)

A recent name change has resulted in Malaysian Airlines System (MAS) changing to its present title of Malaysia Airlines. With the suspension in 1971 of the joint Malaysia-Singapore Airlines agreement the airline was set up by government decree as the national carrier. The initial route network was mainly domestic, with only six international destinations being served by a fleet of Britten-Norman Islanders, Fokker F-27s and Boeing 737s. From its base at Kuala Lumpur's Subang International airport the airline strove to build up its international routes, and to do so acquired a wide bodied fleet of A-300s, DC-10s, and Boeing 747s. It now has a network spanning most of Asia where the A-300s and DC-10s are utilised, and to Australia, Europe and the USA using Jumbos. Looking to the future, ten A-330s have been ordered. Twelve Boeing 737-200s are in use, the first being delivered as long ago as 1972, whilst a substantial number of other variants are on order as replacements. These include one series -300, twenty -400s and six -500s. The present colour scheme was adopted in 1987 and comprises a red and dark blue cheatline below the window line separating the white upper and grey lower fuselage. Dark blue Malaysia titling is on the upper fuselage, whilst on the white fin is the airline's red and dark blue Kalantan Kite logo. The ICAO callsign is 'MALAYSIA'.

Photographed at Kuala Lumpur's Subang airport soon after the application of the present colour scheme is Boeing 737-200 9M-MBM. (Robbie Shaw)

## MALEV (MA/MAH)

Malev is Hungary's national carrier which in recent years has broken with tradition and taken delivery of western equipment in the shape of a BAe-146 and Boeing 737s, with 767s on order. The airline began operations in 1946 under the name Maszovlet, changing to its present title in 1954. From its base at Budapest services are operated to most European countries in addition to a few Middle East destinations. The modest fleet comprises Tupolev Tu-134s and Tu-154s, though the former are to be retired when 737 deliveries are completed. Three 737-200s were leased from Guiness-Peat at the end of 1988 and three series -300s are being acquired

from the same source. The present livery was introduced in late 1990 and is based on a white fuselage apart from the tip of the nose and rear portion which are dark blue. On the rear fuselage the blue extends to cover the whole of the fin, upon which are three diagonal stripes in the colours of the national flag, red, white and green. Dark blue titling appears on the forward upper fuselage. The ICAO callsign is 'MALEV'.

Malev's first Boeing 737-300, HA-LED was photographed on approach to Heathrow as flight MA610 from Budapest. (Robbie Shaw)

# MIDWAY AIRLINES

Midway Airlines was formed in late 1979 to operate scheduled services from Chicago's Midway airport to a number of destinations, most of which were in the north-eastern United States. The network soon spread to Florida, and in 1985 it took over Air Florida, including that airline's routes which entailed a second centre of operations at Miami. Midway's fleet comprised a considerable number of DC-9s of different variants, from the elderly series -10s to the brand new MD-87s and -88s, along with a few Boeing 737-200s. Feeder services were undertaken by Midway Commuter using Dornier 228s and Embraer 120 Brasilias. Unfortunately the airline ceased operations at the end of 1991 due to financial problems, and a hoped for take-over by Northwest Airlines failed. Midway's livery consisted of an all-white fuselage apart from a red belly and a thin black pinstripe running from the nose at wing root level, then sweeping up the leading edge of the fin. The red belly also swept up to encompass the rear fuselage and tail, where the company motif of twin white arrowheads was located. Large red Midway titling covered the whole of the forward fuselage.

Captured on take-off from Miami is Boeing 737-200 N721ML, an aircraft which was absorbed into Midway's fleet with the acquisition of Air Florida. (Robbie Shaw)

## MONARCH AIRLINES (ZB/MON)

An airline well established in the holiday charter market is Luton-based Monarch Airlines. The company was formed in 1967, initially using Bristol Britannias and Boeing 720s to carry customers for its parent company Cosmos. In the past few years Monarch has inaugurated a few scheduled services to several popular holiday destinations, including Alicante, Larnaca, Malaga, Malta, Menorca and Tenerife. Monarch operates a predominantly Boeing fleet, using 737s and 757s, with two 767s on order. Two Airbus A-300s were leased out to Australian carrier Compass, although since that company ceased operations these aircraft have been returned, and

a further four of this type are on order. Monarch's 737 inventory currently comprises eleven series -300s, most of which are leased out to other companies, including EuroBerlin France. The colour scheme comprises an all-white fuselage broken by a yellow (upper) and black (lower) cheatline, with black titling on the upper cabin. The company's black crowned 'M' logo is featured on the white fin. The airline's ICAO callsign is 'MONARCH'.

Illustrated making a perfect touchdown at Luton is Boeing 737-300 G-EURP. (Robbie Shaw)

## NOVAIR INTERNATIONAL

Novair International acquired the name in 1988, having previously been known as Cal-Air International. The name change followed the sale of the British Airways shareholding and that airline's take-over of British Caledonian, which entailed the renaming of the BA charter subsidiary from British Airtours to Caledonian. From its base at Gatwick Novair used three DC-10s on IT charter flights to a number of destinations, principally within Europe. Three Boeing 737-400s were ordered to supplement the DC-10s, the first two arrived in March and April of 1989. Unfortunately their arrival coincided with a downturn in traffic and, after a short period in use,

both aircraft were offered for sale. Novair's parent company, the Rank Organisation, also tried to dispose of the airline, however no buyer was forthcoming for either the 737s or the airline, which ceased operations in May 1991. The innovative colour scheme had a white fuselage bisected by a broad red band running diagonally from underneath the nose to the upper rear fuselage, broken only by a gap forward of the wing root for the blue Novair titling. The white tail had a slightly swept back blue five-pointed star on it.

Climbing out of Gatwick is Boeing 737-400 G-BOPK. (Robbie Shaw)

## OLYMPIC AIRWAYS (OA/OAL)

The Greek national carrier was founded in 1957, and as a wholly-owned government carrier was given the amazing protection of being the only airline in the country, with no competition permitted! Initial operations were with Douglas products, the DC-3, DC-4 and DC-6, the latter being used on international services to London, Paris and Rome, with Frankfurt and Zurich being added soon afterwards. The airline's first jet was the Comet 4B which was used on the prestige European routes. Transatlantic services to New York commenced in 1966 using Boeing 707s, whilst 727s replaced the Comets. On the domestic front YS-11s and Boeing 737s were introduced, though the former have since been transferred to the Greek Air Force. Airbus A-300s are now used alongside the 727s on European routes whilst Boeing 747 Jumbo jets have replaced 707s on USA and Far East services. Olympic received eleven 737-200s, the first arrived in 1975, and six 737-400s are being delivered to replace the 727s. The Olympic colour scheme, unchanged for many years, comprises a dark blue cheatline and tail. The famous six Olympic rings are superimposed on the tail. The upper fuselage is white with dark blue titling and a stylised pennant of the Greek flag, with the lower fuselage and belly in light grey. The ICAO callsign is 'OLYMPIC'.

Boeing 737-200 SX-BCE named 'Dionysus' on final approach to Athens airport as dusk rapidly approaches. (Robbie Shaw)

The first of six Boeing 737-400s, SX-BKA 'Delfini' was delivered to the airline in September 1991, complete with revised livery. The dark blue tail, still containing the Olympic rings, is now a slightly lighter shade similar to royal blue, whilst the cheatline has been completely revised and is now light blue. This is bordered by an upper dark blue pinstripe, and yellow and red lower pinstripes. The pennant-style flag on the upper fuselage has given way to a conventional one. (Robbie Shaw)

## ROYAL AIR MAROC (AT/RAM)

Royal Air Maroc was formed in 1953 after a merger between Air Atlas and Air Maroc. Initial operations were conducted using Junkers Ju-52s which were soon replaced by DC-3s. As with the national airlines of many former French colonies, the Caravelle was selected, and entered service in 1960 on the Casablanca-Paris route. The airline's fleet today is predominantly Boeing orientated, with 737s, 727s and 757s on regional and European routes. Two elderly 707s and two 747s are also in use. Royal Air Maroc is an established 737 operator with seven series -200s in use, the first of which was delivered in 1975. Three -400s and -500s are also in use

with four -300s on order. The airline's livery is based on the colours of the national flag and consists of a green and red cheatline which separates the white fuselage from the belly, which is either grey or natural metal, depending on the aircraft type. The white tail is decorated with a green shooting star with a large red trail, below which are the letters 'RAM'. The red fuselage titling is in English on the starboard side and Arabic on the port. The ICAO callsign is 'MAROCAIR'.

Photographed about to land at Heathrow in December 1991, newly-delivered Boeing 737-500 CN-RMW. (Robbie Shaw)

## ROYAL BRUNEI AIRLINES (BI/RBA)

Royal Brunei Airlines was formed in 1974, and the following year commenced services from the capital, Bandar Seri Begawan to regional Asian destinations. A few Boeing 737-200s were the mainstay of the airline until the acquisition in 1986 of the first of three Boeing 757s, all of which have a lavish internal decor. Since the 757s were introduced the airline has commenced services to Europe, including a London/Gatwick service. These services are now operated by recently-delivered Boeing 767s, whilst the 737s have now been disposed of. With the introduction of the long range 757s

and 767s a new colour scheme has been introduced, featuring a yellow lower belly separated from the rest of the white fuselage by yellow and black pinstripes. The whole arrangement sweeps up to encompass the fin where the brown national symbol is superimposed. Black titling and the national flag is on the forward upper fuselage. The ICAO callsign is 'BRUNEI'.

Wearing the airline's old colour scheme is Boeing 737-200 V8-UEB about to land at Hong Kong's Kai Tak airport. (Robbie Shaw)

# SABENA BELGIAN WORLD AIRLINES (SN/SAB)

Sabena-Belgian World Airlines was formed in 1923 to succeed the airline Syndicate National pour l'Étude des Transports Aerienne (SNETA). The name Sabena comes simply from the initials Société Anonyme Belge d'Exploitation de la Navigation Aerienne. Initially services to Switzerland and France were consolidated before further expansion throughout Europe was undertaken. During the Second World War the airline moved its headquarters to the Belgian Congo (now Zaire). When hostilities ceased the airline returned to Brussels where a New York service was inaugurated initially using DC-4s, which were eventually replaced by the DC-6B and DC-7C. The first jet equipment was the Boeing 707 for use on transatlantic routes, whilst in common with a number of European airlines the Caravelle was selected for routes within that continent.

Today the Boeing 737 is the backbone of the fleet, with thirteen series -200s, seven -300s and three -400s, whilst the first of eleven -500s has recently been delivered. Smaller numbers of A-310s, DC-10s and Boeing 747s are also in use, and five A-340s are on order. The current livery was introduced in 1984 to coincide with the entry into service of the A-310s. The white upper fuselage contains blue titling and the national flag, whilst the light blue cheatline, trimmed either side by matching pinstripes, runs the length of the fuselage. The lower fuselage is grey, and the light blue tail has a large white disc which contains the stylised 'S' notif. The ICAO callsign is 'SABENA'.

On final approach to runway 27L at Heathrow is OO-SDW a Boeing 737-300. (Robbie Shaw)

## SOUTHWEST AIRLINES (JAPAN) (NU/SWL)

Not to be confused with the US carrier of the same name, Southwest Airlines is a Japanese regional airline based at Naha, Okinawa. Formed in 1967, the airline operates services throughout the Ryuku Islands off Japan's southwest coast. The fleet consists of DHC Twin Otters, NAMC YS-11s and Boeing 737-200s. Eight of the latter are on the airline's inventory. The airline colour scheme has a bright orange fuselage cheatline which broadens at the rear to include the base of the fin. This is trimmed by a lower red stripe. The top of the fin also has a swept up orange portion, below which is the red circular 'SWAL' motif and letters on a white background. The belly is grey and the upper fuselage white, with black titling in Japanese and English. The airline's ICAO callsign is 'NANSEI'.

Taxying for take-off at Naha is Boeing 737-200 JA8445. (Robbie Shaw)

# SOUTHWEST AIRLINES (USA) (WN/SWA)

Like its Japanese namesake, Dallas-based Southwest Airlines was formed in 1967, though under the name Air Southwest. The present name was adopted in 1971, and the carrier operates an extensive route network throughout the south west USA, although it does have a few destinations in other corners of the nation. Southwest has a large fleet of Boeing 737s, the only type on its inventory. At the time of writing this comprised; forty-six series -200s, fifty-three -300s with nine more on order, whilst about half of the forty-eight -500 series on order have been delivered. The airline's livery has a mustard-coloured fuselage which is separated from the red belly by a white pinstripe. These two colours continue along the fuselage, to run

vertically up the tail where they are joined by an orange stripe which covers the lower half of the rudder. The Southwest titling is in white on the leading edge of the fin, and the fuselage colours are repeated on the engine cowlings. The ICAO callsign is 'SOUTH-WEST'.

The colour scheme worn by Boeing 737-300 N334SW about to land at Detroit Metropolitan airport is definitely non-standard! This is one of two aircraft where the whale 'Shamu' is overpainted on the fuselage, advertising the Texas Sea World leisure complex. (Robbie Shaw).

## TAN SAHSA (TX/TAN & SH/SHA)

TAN (Transportes Aereos Nacionales) and SAHSA (Servicio Aereo de Honduras) are two modest Honduran carriers which maintain a close co-operation. Both operate regional services, the former using one Boeing 737-200 and two Lockhead Electras, whilst the latter employs three DC-3s, two Boeing 737-200s and one 727. The close co-operation has extended to the use of a leased Boeing 737-200, N501AV wearing the titling of both airlines, which was photographed on a service to Miami in May 1990. (Robbie Shaw)

## THAI AIRWAYS

Thai Airways was a government-owned domestic airline which was formed in 1947 as the result of a merger between Pacific Overseas Airlines and Siamese Airways. A large number of routes linked the capital Bangkok with some twenty destinations within the country. Although formed as a domestic airline, expansion brought the introduction of services to Laos, Malaysia, Singapore and Vietnam. An 1959 agreement with SAS brought about the formation of a subsidiary, Thai International, which was formed to develop and operate international routes. During the 1980s Thai International became extremely successful, and in 1988 actually took over Thai Airways, the airline of which it was once a subsidiary! At that time

Thai Airways was operating a fleet of Shorts SD-330s and 360s, four Boeing 737-200s and two Airbus A-310s. Thai Airways had an imaginative colour scheme, the white fuselage being broken by a magenta/orange/magenta cheatline trimmed in gold, commencing below the cockpit then sweeping up over the wing along the upper cabin. The white fin has a magenta orange and gold stylised Royal Orchid with titling underneath – in English on the port side and Thai script on the starboard.

Photographed being pushed back from its stand at Bangkok is Boeing 737-200 HS-TBD. This shot was taken only a few months prior to the take-over. (Robbie Shaw)

## TRANSAVIA AIRLINES (HV/TRA)

Formed in 1965 and partly-owned by the national carrier KLM, Transavia concentrates on a charter network to the main Mediterranean holiday resorts. The airline is also involved in leasing agreements and its aircraft, usually still retaining at least part of their Transavia livery, are frequently seen operating on behalf of other carriers. Transavia has recently inaugurated an Amsterdam-London/Gatwick scheduled service which is proving popular. The airline uses an all-Boeing 737 fleet, a mix of both -200 and -300 series, though numbers vary due to leasing agreements, and two Boeing 757s are on order. The mainly white colour scheme features a stylised 'T' on the forward lower fuselage, streaming back from which is a black band separated by green and red pinstripes. The black Transavia titling runs vertically up the white fin, and the belly is grey. This scheme however has recently been revised to omit the black and red, whilst the green is now a slightly lighter shade. The ICAO callsign is 'TRANSAVIA'.

Photographed on short finals to Gatwick is Boeing 737-200 PH-TVH. (Robbie Shaw)

## TRANS BRASIL (TR/TBA)

Trans Brasil was formed in 1955 under the name Sadia using a DC-3 to carry fresh meat. The following year scheduled services were commenced, and in 1972 the airline adopted its present title. From its base at Brasilia, the nation's capital, the airline operates an all-Boeing fleet which includes 707s, 727s, 737s and 767s. Apart from Miami and Orlando the airline's route network does not spread beyond Brazil. The airline currently operates some fifteen leased 737s, four of which are series -400s, the remainder -300s. The attractive livery is centred on the airline's rainbow-coloured fin, the remainder of the aircraft being white with blue titling on the lower forward fuselage. The airline's ICAO callsign is 'TRANSBRASIL'.

Photographed on push-back at Sao Paulo is Boeing 737-300 PT-TEC. (J. Oliveira)

## TRANS EUROPEAN AIRWAYS

Formed in 1970, Trans European Airways operated inclusive tour charter flights from its Brussels base. Operations were started with a leased Boeing 720, and subsequently 707s and an Airbus A-300 have been used. In recent years the airline has established other charter arms in France, Italy, Switzerland and the UK, these being known as TEA France etc. The Boeing 737-300 was the aircraft chosen to equip the fleet of the parent company and its subsidiaries, though aircraft were swapped between the operators from time to time. In September 1991 TEA operations ceased due to financial difficulties,

the knock-on effect had the same effect on TEA (UK) and TEA (France) operations. However TEA (Italy) and Switzerland continue to operate. The colour scheme of the airline and its subsidiaries featured a white fuselage with bold TEA titling forward of the wing root, and a dark blue tail with white titling surrounded by a circle of gold stars.

Illustrated taxying at Geneva is Boeing 737-300 OO-LTJ. (Robbie Shaw)

## TUNIS AIR (TU/TAR)

The Tunisian national airline, Tunis Air, was formed in 1948 with an agreement between the Tunisian government and Air France. Using a single Douglas DC-3 services commenced from Tunis to Algiers and Paris, and following the acquisition of a DC-4 expansion included Lyon, Marseilles and Rome. Not surprisingly, the first jet selected was the Sud-Aviation Caravelle, which soon featured on the airline's European network, whilst Nord 262s were bought for domestic use. Tunis Air now has an extensive network in Europe and the Middle East, using Boeing 727s, 737s and Airbus A-320s, with the flagship of the fleet being a single A-300. The A-320s are slowly replacing the 727s. Four Boeing 737-200s are in use with two

-500s on order. The old airline livery has twin red cheatlines running the length of the fuselage below the window line. The lower fuselage is light grey and the upper is white with black titling in both English and Arabic. The white tail has a red stylised 'TA', with white leaping gazelle superimposed on the 'A'. In 1991 an attractive new livery introduced a white scheme with red titling and a large leaping gazelle on the fin with trailing pinstripes, all in red. The ICAO callsign is 'TUNAIR'.

Featuring the old livery at Zurich is Boeing 737 TS-IOE named 'Zarzis'. (Robbie Shaw)

## UNITED AIRLINES (UA/UAL)

United Airlines is one of the largest airlines in the US, and is steadily expanding in Europe with the acquisition of routes and aircraft from Pan American. The airline experienced similar expansion in the Pacific area in 1986, again at Pan American's expense. The large fleet of over 400 aircraft consists mainly of Boeing products, with large numbers of 727s, 737s and 757s on domestic services, with 747s, 767s and McDonnell-Douglas DC-10s on both domestic and intercontinental routes. United was an early customer for the 737-200, of which it currently has seventy-four. The series -300 is operated in even greater numbers, with 101 on the inventory, and the bulk of thirty-five -500s on order have been delivered. The colour scheme has a white fuselage bisected by an orange/red/blue cheatline, with the same colours forming a stylised 'U' logo on the white fin. Black titling is on the upper cabin and the belly is highly polished natural metal. The airline's ICAO callsign is 'UNITED'.

Against stormy skies Boeing 737-300 N336UA is about to land at Buffalo, New York. (Robbie Shaw)